IRENAEUS
Against Heresies

CLEMENT OF ALEXANDRIA

The Exhortation to the Greeks
and
Quis Dives Salvetur?

STUDY OUTLINES 2 & 3

Ford Lewis Battles

PICKWICK PUBLICATIONS
Allison Park, Pennsylvania

Copyright © 1993 by Marion D. Battles

Published by

Pickwick Publications
4137 Timberlane Drive
Allison Park, PA 15101-2932
USA

Printed on Acid Free Paper in the United States of America

Library of Congress Cataloging-in-Publication Data

Battles, Ford Lewis
      [Selections. 1993]
      Irenaeus, Against heresies ; Clement of Alexandria, The
exhortation to the Greeks ; and, Quis dives salvetur? / Ford
Lewis Battles.
            p. cm. -- (Study outlines ; #2-3)
      ISBN 1-55635-019-8
      1. Theology--Early church, ca. 30-600--Outlines, syllabi, etc.
2. Irenaeus, Saint, Bishop of Lyon. Adversus haereses. 3. Clement,
of Alexandria, Saint, ca. 150-ca. 215. Protrepticus. 4. Clement,
of Alexandria, Saint, ca. 150-ca. 215. Quis dives salvetur?
5. Christian literature, Early--Outlines, syllabi, etc.   I. Title.
II. Series: Study outline (Allison Park, Pa.) ; 2-3.
      BR65.I63A355   1993
      239'. 3--dc20   93-22092
                                                                CIP

CONTENTS

STRUCTURE: *AGAINST HERESIES*

IRENAEUS

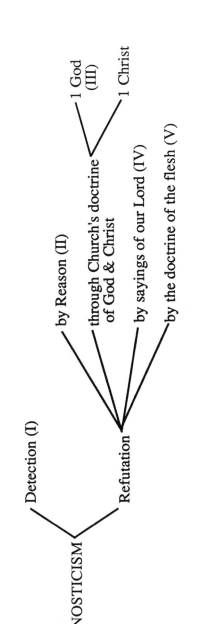

GNOSTICISM

Detection (I)

Refutation

by Reason (II)

through Church's doctrine
of God & Christ

by sayings of our Lord (IV)

by the doctrine of the flesh (V)

1 God
(III)

1 Christ

STRUCTURE: *AGAINST HERESIES*

IRENAEUS

God, Christ, Scripture (OT & NT) = Unity

Against Gnostics, Irenaeus asserts UNITY

IIIa	One God
IIIb	One Christ (no docetism or mere adoptionism)
IV	One Bible (unity of OT & NT)
V	One Man (unity of body & soul in life hereafter)

Irenaeus
Against Heresies

(Note: The main divisions are as suggested by Irenaeus (*AH*, 5.19. 2) and given by Quasten, *Patrology*, 1.289. The analysis of Books III-V are from *Sources Chrétiennes*, vols. 34, 100)

FIRST DIVISION: *The Detection of the Gnostic Heresy (Book I)*

Preface

THIRD DIVISION: *Refutation of Gnostic Teaching from the Sayings of the Lord (Book IV)*

Preface: After the Apostles' Teaching, the Words of Christ

Part I: The Unity of the Two Testaments Proved by the Clear Words of Christ (1-19)

"You have only one Father, him who is in heaven." (1:1)
"I praise thee, O Father, Lord of heaven and earth." (2.1)
"If you have believed Moses, you should believe me also." (2.3)
Heaven, throne of God; earth, His footstool; Jerusalem, City of the Great King (2.5)
Heaven and earth will pass away. (3.1)
Jerusalem was forsaken. (4.1)
"He is not God of the dead, but of the living." (5.2)
"Abraham has seen my day." (5.3)
"No one knows the Father..." (6.1)
Abraham knew the Father (7.1)
Abraham and the prophets in the Kingdom of Heaven (8.1)
The observance of the Sabbath (8.2)
Things new and old (9.1)
Greater than the temple and than Jonah and Solomon (9.2)
The Law, God's Word. (9.3)
The Son of God implanted in the Scriptures (10.1)
The prophets desired to see Christ (11.1)
The essentials of the Law (12.1)
"Do what they say" (12.4)
"Keep the Commandments." (12.5)
"I have come not to abolish, but to fulfill" (13.1)
"I no longer call you slaves" (13.4)
God has need of nothing (13.4)

Part III: The Unity of the Two Testaments Proved by the Parables of Christ (36-41)

FOURTH DIVISION: *Defense of The Resurrection of the Flesh (Book V)*

Preface: The Remaining Teaching of the Lord and the Epistles of Paul

Part I: The Resurrection of the Flesh proved by the Epistles of Paul (1-14)

of the resurrection of the flesh (2. 2-3)
B. The Resurrection of the flesh, work of the power of
    God (3-5)
  1. "My grace is sufficient for you" (3.1) [2 Cor.
    12:8]
  2. God can quicken the flesh and the flesh can be
    quickened by God (3. 2-3)
  3. The pretended "Father" imagined by the heretics
    is only an impotent or jealous one. (4.1-2)
  4. Biblical examples illustrating the quickening
    power of God (5: 1-2)
    a. Longevity of the first man
    b. Translation of Enoch and Elijah into paradise
    c. Saving of Jonah cast into the sea
    d. Three children in the fiery furnace
C. Pauline texts attesting the resurrection of the flesh
    (6-8)
  1. May your whole being—spirit, soul, body—be
    kept faultless for the coming of the Lord Jesus"!
    (6.1) [1 Thess. 5:23]
  2. The flesh, "temple of God" and "member of
    Christ," could not sleep utterly in death. (6.2) [1
    Cor. 3:16/1 Cor. 6:15].
  3. The bodily resurrection of Christ, earnest of our
    bodily resurrection (6.2-7.1) [1 Cor. 6:13f/Rom.
    8:11]
  4. The flesh will be raised up, incorruptible, glori-
    ous, spiritual (7.1-2) [1 Cor. 15:42-44,46]
  5. The spirit given for believers as earnest of the
    future resurrection (7.2-8.1) [1 Cor. 13.9, 12:
    Eph. 1:13f]
  6. "Spirituals" and "physicals" (8.2-3) [1 Cor. 2:15;
    3:1/1 Cor. 3:3]
D. True sense of the Pauline phrase "Flesh and Blood
    cannot inherit the Kingdom of God" (9-14) [1
    Cor. 15:50]
  1. "Flesh and blood" (9.1-2) [1 Cor. 15:50/1 Thess.
    5:23]
  2. Feebleness of the flesh and readiness of the spirit

(9.2) [Mt. 26:41]
3. Image of what is earthly and image of what is heavenly (9.3) [1 Cor. 15:48f/Rom.6:4]
4. The flesh possessed as an inheritance by the Spirit (9.4) [Mt. 5:5]
5. The ingrafting of the Spirit (10.1-2) [Rom. 11:17, 24]
6. "You are not in the flesh, but in the Spirit" (10.2) [Rom. 8:8-14]
7. Works of the flesh and works of the Spirit (11.1) [Gal. 5:19, 22]
8. The unrighteous will not inherit the Kingdom of God (11.1-2) [1 Cor. 6:9-11]
9. "Breath of Life" and "Quickening Spirit" (12.1-3) [1 Cor. 15:45f]
10. "Mortify your earthly members" (12.3-4) [Col. 3:5, 9f]
11. Cures and resurrections brought about by Christ (12.5-13.2)
12. "What is corruptible must put on incorruption" (13.3-5) [1 Cor. 15:53-55; Phil. 3:20f; 2 Cor. 5:4f; 2 Cor. 4:10f; 3-3; Phil. 3:10f;.1 Cor. 15:32, 13-21]
13. "You have been reconciled by his fleshly body" (14.1-4) [Col. 1:21, 7, 13, 15]

Part II: The Identity of God the Creator and God the Father proved by three facts of the life of Christ (15-24)

A. The healing of the man born blind (15-16.2) [Jn. 9:1-7]
1. The resurrection promised by God the Creator (15-1) [Is. 26:19; 66.13f; Ez. 37:1-10, 12-14; Is. 65:22]
2. The case of the man born blind, revelation of the creative action of the Word at the beginning of humanity. (15.2-3) [Jn. 9:1-7; cf. Gen. 2:7; Jer.

1:5; Gal. 1:15]
3. A single earth, a single God, a single Word.
(15.4-16.2)
B. The Crucifixion (16.3-20)
1. The disobedience by the wood restored by the
obedience on the wood (16.3) [Phil. 2:8]
2. The forgiveness of sins paid by the one to whom
we were debtors (17.1-3) [Mt. 6:12; 9:2, 6]
3. The "economy" of the wood prefigured by Elisha
(17.4)
4. The Word set forth by its own creation (18.1-2)
5. The Word came into its own domain (18.2-3)
6. Contradictions of the heretical systems over
against the unity of the Church's teaching (19.1-
20.2)
C. The Temptation of Christ (21-24) [Mt. 4:2ff]
1. The victory of Christ over the devil, replica of the
fall of Adam (21.1) [cf. Gen. 3:15]
2. Christ triumphant over the devil to the help of
the Commandments of the God of the Law
(21.2-22.1) [Dt. 8:3; Ps. 91:llf; Dt. 6:13]
3. The Christians instruction in their duties by these
same commandments of the God of the Law
(22.2)
4. The lying devil since the beginning (23.1-2)
5. The earthly Kingdom established by God, not by
the devil (24.1-4)

Part III: **The Identity of God the Creator and God the
Father proved by the Teaching of the Scrip-
tures on the End of Times (25-36)**

A. The Antichrist (25-30)
1. The apostasy of Antichrist and his pretension to
be worshiped as God in the temple at Jerusalem.
(25.1-5) [2 Thess 2:3f; Mt. 24:15-17, 21; Dan.
7:7f, 20-25; 2 Thess. 2:8-12; Jn. 5:43; Dan.
8:11f, 23-25; 9:37]

2. The division of the royal kingdom and the final triumph of Christ (26.1-2) [Rev. 17:12-14; Mt. 12:25; Dan. 2:33f, 41-45]
3. The righteous judgment of God against Satan and all those who share in his apostasy (26.2-28.2) [2 Thess. 2:10-12]
4. The figure of the name of Antichrist announcement of the recapitulation of all apostasy in his person (28.2-29.2) [Rev. 13:2-18]
5. The figure of the name of Antichrist—can that name be recognized with certainty up to now? (30.1-4)
B. The Resurrection of the Righteous (31-36)
1. Progressive steps in the progress of the righteous on the road to the heavenly life (31.1-2)
2. The kingdom of the righteous, fulfilment of the promise made by God to the patriarchs (32.1-2)
3. The inheritance of the earth announced by Christ and promised by the blessing of Jacob and by Isaiah (33.1-4) [Mt. 26:27-29; Lk. 14:12f; Gen. 27:27-29; Is. 11:6-9; 65:25]
4. Israel reestablished in its land, in work to share in the blessing of the Lord (34.1-3) [Is. 26:19; Ez. 37:12-14; 28:25f; Jer. 16:14f/Is. 30:25f; Gen. 9:27; Is. 58:14/Is. 6:11; Dan. 7:27; 12:13/Lk. 12:37f/Rev. 20:6]
5. Jerusalem gloriously rebuilt (34.4-35.2) [Is. 31:9-32.1; 54:11-14; 65:18-22/Is. 6:11f; 13:9; 26:10; 65:21/Baruch 4:36-5:9]
6. After the Kingdom of the righteous: the Jerusalem from above and the Kingdom of the Father (35.2-36.2) [Rev. 20:11-21: 6; Gal. 4:26; 1 Cor. 7:31]
7. Conclusion: one single Father, one single Son, one single human race. (36.3)

Analysis of Book V vols. 152, 153 of *Sources Chrétiennes*

FIFTH DIVISION: *Proof of the Apostolic Preaching*

Note: This outline is a composite of Quasten, J. P. Smith (*Ancient Christian Writers*, 16), and my own headings. Section numbers (in parentheses) were originally assigned by Harnack.

I. Introduction

    A. Preface to Marcianus: the Way of Life (1)
    B. Man and His Duty to God (2-3)
       1. Man's holiness must be total: of both soul and body (2)
       2. The Rule of Faith
          a. our baptism for remission of sins in the name of Father, Son, and H/S—seal of eternal life and rebirth to God
          b. God is one: Creator and Ruler over all things

II. Part I: Essential Content of the Christian Faith (4-41)

    A. The Triune God (4-8)
       1. Origin of creatures (4)
       2. The Trinity and creatures (5)
       3. The Three Articles of the Faith
          a. God the Father, uncreated, beyond grasp, invisible, one God the Maker of all
          b. Word of God, Son of God, Christ Jesus our Lord
             (1) shown forth by the prophets
             (2) through Him all things were made
             (3) in the end of times, for the recapitulation of all things, is to become a man among men, visible and tangible, in order to abolish death and bring to light life, and communion of God and man.
          c. Holy Spirit
             (1) through whom the prophets prophesied

c. Christ in Glory. He Himself redeemed us (Is.
   50:8f; 2:17) (88)
2. The calling of the Gentiles (89-97)
   a. The Spirit supersedes the Law (Is. 43:18ff)
      (89)
   b. Newness of Spirit. The New Covenant (Jer.
      31:31ff- cf. Rom. 7:6; Heb. 8:9ff) (90)
   c. The Gentiles heirs to the promises (Is. 17:7f;
      65:1 (91-92)
   d. The Gentiles to be a holy people (Hos.. 2:23-
      1:10; cf.Rom. 9:25f; Ez.11:19f) (93)
   e. Church more fruitful than Synagogue (Is.
      54:1; Gal. 4:27 (94)
   f. The Gentiles supplant Israel. (Dt. 28:44;
      32:31) (95)
   g. We have no need of the Law (Ex. 20f; cf. I
      Cor. 13:10; Hos. 6:6; Is. 66:3; Joel 2:32)
      (96)
   h. Nearness of almighty aid (Baruch 3:29-4:1).
      (97)

IV. Conclusion (98-100)

A. Summation (98).

B. Denial of the Gnostic belief in another God than the
   Creator (99-100)

C. Subscription: Praise to the Trinity (100)

Clement of Alexandria
The Exhortation to the Greeks

A comparison of the translation of G. W. Butterworth, *Clement of Alexandria* with an English translation. Loeb Classical Library (1919), and A. Cleveland Coxe, *Ante-Nicene Fathers* (rev. ed.) (1885).

Chapter One: Exhortation to Abandon the Impious Mysteries of Idolatry for the Adoration of the Divine Word and God the Father

I. Minstrels of legend and their wonderful deeds
   A. Arion, Amphion, Orpheus.
   B. The marvelous song sung by Eunomus and the Pythian grasshopper.

II. How in the world is it that you have given credence to worthless legends while the bright face of truth is regarded with unbelieving eyes?
   A. In your hands the records of these evils have become dramas and the actors gladden your hearts.
   B. Let us shut them up Helicon and bring down truth with wisdom to God's holy mountain.
      1. Let truth shine everywhere to point them to salvation.
      2. Let them forsake Helicon to dwell in Zion.
   C. This Eunomus of mine sings the new music, that is the new song.

III. In my opinion such men, and yet unworthy of the name
of man, are deceivers who under cover of music,
have outraged human life.
A. They were the first to lead men to idolatry.
B. But such is not my song, whlch has come to loose us
from the slavery of the daemons.
1. It recalls to heaven those that had been cast pros-
trate to the earth.
2. It alone has tamed man, the most intractable of
beasts.
C. The silly are stocks and stones, and still more senseless is a way steeped in ignorance.
1. Scripture proof: Mt 3:9, Lk 3:8.
D. But, God did, in His compassion, raise up out of
those stones, that is the Gentiles, a seed of piety
sensitive to virtue.
E. Other figurative images adduced to demonstrate
God's Compassion.
1. The "offspring of vipers" (Mt 3:7, Lk 3:7) who in
following the Word becomes a man of God.
2. "Wolves" (Mt 7:15), clothed in sheepskins and
all such other savage beasts transformed by the
heavenly song. (I Tim 6:11)

IV. See how mighty is this new song! Those who were
dead revived when they heard the song.
A. Furthermore, this song composed the entire creation
into melodious order that the universe might be in
harmony with it.
B. What is more, this pure song reduced this whole
harmony in accordance with the fatherly purpose of
God, which David earnestly sought.
C. And he who is of David, and yet before him, the
Word of God arranged in harmonious order this
great world and the little world of man, body and
soul together.
1. The Lord fashioned man a beautiful instrument,
after His own image .

V. What then, is the purpose of this instrument, the Word
of God, and the New Song?
   A. To reveal God to foolish men, to reconclle disobedient sons to the Father.
   B. The Lord promises the Kingdom of heaven as reward for our discipleship.
      1. The only joy He has of us is that we are saved.
   C. You have then God's promise. Partake of His grace!

VI. And do not suppose that my song of salvation is new.
For it was from the beginning (Ps 60:3, 110; Jn 1:1).
   A. Neither the Phrygians, nor the Arcadians, nor the
   Egyptians existed before this world: but we were
   before the foundation of the world because we were
   destined to be in Him.
   B. We are the rational creatures of the Word of God, on
   whose account we date from the beginning.
   C. The Word, then, that is the Christ, is the cause of our
   being long ago and of our well-being.
   D. Thls Word appeared but lately in His own person to
   men.
      1. This is the New Song, the manifestation of the
      Word that was in the beginning and before the
      beginning.
   E. Not long ago the pre-existent Saviour appeared on
   earth as our teacher .
      1. He who gave us life in the beginning taught us
      how to live, that as God He might supply us
      wlth life everlasting.

VII. This was not the first time He pitied us for our error.
But now by His appearing He has rescued us, when we
were on the point of perishing.
   A. For the crawling reptile makes slaves of men from
   their birth, binding them to his side to idols, etc.,
   until they together suffer corruption.
   B. Therefore, our rescuer and helper is one also, namely, the Lord, who now invites us plainly to salvation.

C. Let us then, in obedience to the apostolic precept,
   flee from "the prlnce of the power of the air" (Eph.
   2:2).
   1. And let us take refuge with the Saviour, who
      even now exhorts men to salvation.
D. By signs and wonders He has ever shown His love.
   1. In Egypt through Moses.
   2. Later through Isaiah and all the prophets by a
      way appealing to reason.
E. The Saviour uses many tones and devices in working
   for the salvation of men.
   1. His threats are warnings.
   2. His rebukes for converting, etc.
F. But if you do not believe the prophets the Lord himself shall speak to you. (Phil 2: 6-7).
   1. "And the Word Himself now speaks to you plain-
      ly, putting to shame your unbelief . . . having
      become man, in order that such as you may
      learn from man how it is even possible for man
      to become a god!"

VIII. Then is it not monstrous my friends, that, while God
   is exhorting us to virtue, we put off our salvation?
   A. Does not John also invite us to salvation?
      1. Who then is John?
      2. John is a forerunner, and the voice (Is 40:3) is a
         forerunner of the Word.
      3. By reason of this voice, the barren is fruitless no
         longer.
   B. This fecundity the angel's voice foretold. That
      voice was also a forerunner, inasmuch as it brought
      glad tidings to a barren woman (Lk 1:7-13), as John
      did to the desert.
      1. These two forerunning voices of the Lord speak
         darkly of the salvation laid up for us.
      2. The Scripture makes this all clear, by referring
         both voices to the same thlng. (Is 54:3): For this
         husband of the barren woman and this husband-
         man of the desert are one and the same.

C. So then by reason of the Word both become mothers, yet even now the words "barren" and "desert" remain for unbelievers.

IX. For this reason John summoned men to prepare for the presence of God, that is, of Christ.

   A. This was also the hidden meaning of the dumbness of Zacharias, that the light of truth, the Word, should break the mystic silence of the dark prophetic sayings, by becoming good tidings.

   B. If you long to see God truly, take part in the purifications meant for Him.

      1. Crown yourself with righteousness and seek diligently after Christ.

   C. For the gates of the Word are gates of reason, opened by the Key of faith.

      1. He who opens this door unveils what is within and shows what we could not have discerned before except we had entered through Christ.

Chapter Two: The Absurdity and Impiety of the Heathen Mysteries and Fables about the Birth and Death of Their Gods.

I. Do not therefore seek diligently after godless sanctuaries; abandon them to the regions of legends now grown old.

   A. All the springs of divination are dead, and stripped of their vain glory, although at a late time, are shown with the fabulous legends to have run dry.

   B. Let also the sanctuaries of Egypt and the Tuscan oracles of the dead be delivered over to darkness.

   C. They are all truly insane devices of unbelieving men.

      1. Not only devices, but also animals have been brought into this godless service.

II. But what if I were to recount the mysteries for you?

   A. I will thoroughly lay bare, in accordance with the principle of truth. the trickery they conceal.

   B. And those so-called gods of yours I shall display, as

it were, on the stage live to the spectators of truth.
1. Dionysus is worshiped by Bacchants with orgies
   by a feast of raw flesh.
2. Demeter and Persephone have come to be the
   subject of a mystic drama.
3. Eleusis celebrates with torches the rape of the
   daughter and the wanderings of the mother.
4. The terms "orgy" and "mystery" must be derived:
   the former from the wrath (*orge*) of Demeter,
   and the latter from the pollution that took place
   in connection with Dionysus. (*musos*)
C. Your mysteries have received the glory of funeral
   honors!
   1. You may also suppose them to be hunting-stories
      (*mytheris*), for most certainly fables of this sort
      hunt after the most barbarous and superstitious
      of men.

III. A curse then upon the man who started this deception
   for mankind, whether it be Dardanus, Eetion, or Midas.
   A. These men I for my part would call originators of
      mischief, seeing that they implanted the mysteries
      in human life to be a seed of evil and corruption.

IV. But now I wlll convict your orgies themselves of being
   full of deception and quackery
   A. And if you have been initiated, you will laugh all the
      more at these fables of yours which have been held
      in honor.
   B. I publish without reserve what has been involved in
      secrecy.

V. The mysteries are revealed.
   A. There is the "foam-born" and "Cyprus born" goddess
      Aphrodite, who received the name Philomedes be-
      cause she was born from those lustful members that
      were cut off from Uranus and did violence to the
      sea.

1. And in rites which celebrate this pleasure of the sea, the initiates bring their coin of tribute to the goddess, as lovers do to a mistress.
B. The mysteries of Demeter commemorate the amorous embraces of Zeus with his mother Demeter, and the wrath of Demeter.
  1. The same rites are performed in honor of Attis and Cybele and the Corybantes.
  2. The sign given to those who are initiated is a serpent drawn over the breast of the votaries, a proof of the licentiousness of Zeus.
C. The mysteries of Dionyus are of a perfectly savage character.
  1. The Titans tore him to pieces, though he was but an infant.
  2. Now Athena made off with the heart of Dionysus, but the Titans boiled his limbs in a caldron.
  3. Later Zeus appeared and plagued the Titans with thunder.
  4. Apollo, the son of Zeus, then carries the mutilated corpse to Parnassus for burial.

VI. A further mystery revealed.
A. If you wish to inspect the orgies of the Corybantes, then know that it is one of fratricide of the worst sort.
  1. The mysteries are, in short, murders and burials.
  2. The priests of these mysteries add a portent to the dismal tale. They believe that wild celery grows out of the blood that flowed from the murdered brother and therefore forbid men to eat it.
  3. The women of Thesmophoria celebrate a similar rite, believing the seeds of the pomegranate to have sprung from the drops of the blood of Dionysus.
  4. Then, this pair of fratricides got possession of the chest in which the phallus of Dionysus was deposited and brought it to Tuscany.

5. There they sojourned and communicated their
   precious teaching of piety, the phallus and the
   chest, to the Tuscans for the purposes of worship.
B. Yet how can we wonder if Tuscans, who are barbari-
   ans, are thus consecrated to base passions, when
   Athenians possess that shameful tale about Demeter?
   1. Demeter becomes exhausted and sits down at a
      well in deep distress.
   2. Baubo offers her a draught of wine and meal,
      which Demeter refuses.
   3. Baubo is deeply hurt and thereupon uncovers her
      secret parts before Demeter.
   4. Demeter is overjoyed at the sight and receives the
      draught.
   5. These are the secret mysteries of the Athenians.

VII. The mysteries are mere custom and vain opinion, and
    it is a deceit of the serpent that men worship when they
    turn towards these sacred initiations that are solemn
    rites without sanctity.
    A. Consider the contents of the mystic chests, sesame
       cakes and balls of salt.
       1. These are their holy things!
       2. Formerly night was a time for silence, but now
          night is for those who are being initiated into the
          tell-tale rites of licentiousness.
       3. Quench the fire, thou priest, for the light convicts
          you.
    B. These are the mysteries of Atheists, who are ignorant
       of the true God.
    C. It is a twofold atheism in which they are entangled.
       1. They are ignorant of the true God, since they do
          not recognize him.
       2. They believe in the existence of beings that have
          no being, and call them gods when they are no
          gods.

VIII. Blessings be upon the Scythian king, whoever he was.
  A. When a countryman of his was imitating the rite of
     the "Mother of the Gods, this king slew him with an
     arrow, on the ground that the man was communicat-
     ing an effeminate disease to his fellow Scythians."
  B. All this makes me amazed how the term atheist has
     been applied to Euhemus, Nicanor, etc.
     1. Even if they did not perceive the truth itself, they
        at least suspected the error.
     2. This suspicion is a living spark of wisdom, and
        no small one, which grows up like a seed into
        truth.

IX. It appears then that atheism and daemon worship are
    the extreme points of stupidity, from which we must
    earnestly endeavor to keep ourselves apart.
  A. Do you not see Moses ordering that no eunuch or
     mutilated man shall enter the assembly, nor the son
     of a harlot (Dt 23:1)?
     1. By the first two he refers in a figure to the atheis-
        tic manner of life.
     2. By the third he refers to the man who lays claim
        to many gods in place of the only real God.
  B. Now there was an innate original communion be-
     tween men and heaven, obscured through ignor-
     ance, but which now has leapt forth instantaneously
     from the darkness.

X. But opinions that are mistaken and deviate from the
   right turned man aside from a heavenly manner and
   stretched him upon the earth.
  A. For some, when they looked at the motion of the
     stars, deified them, giving them the name of gods
     from their running motion.
  B. Others, when gathering the cultivated fruits of plants
     that spring from the earth, deified the fruits of these
     plants.
  C. Others, after reflecting upon the punishments of evil-
     doing, worshiped the very calamities.

D. Even some of the philosophers came to represent as
   deities the types of your emotions.
   1. Some gods arise from the mere circumstances of
      life deified in men's eyes and fashioned in
      bodily form.
E. Finally, there remains that which arises from the divine beneficence shown towards men: since men
   did not understand that it was God who benefited
   them, they invented certain saviors.

XI. These then are the slippery and harmful paths which
    lead away from the truth, dragging man down from
    heaven and overturning him into the pit.
    A. But I wish to display to you the gods themselves and
       whether they really exist, that at last you may cease
       from error and run back again to heaven.
    B. For the Word is living, and he who has been buried
       with Christ is exalted together with God.
    C. The unbelieving are "children of wrath" (Eph 2:3),
       but we are no longer creatures of wrath, for we are
       hastening towards the truth.
       1. Thus, we have now become sons of God thanks
          to the love of the Word of man.
    D. Most of the stories about your gods are legends and
       fictions and many are the records of base men who
       led dissolute lives.
    E. (We must) strip the crowd of deities of those terrify-
       ing and threatening masks of theirs by showing the
       similarity of names.
       1. Zeus has three names.
       2. Athena has five names, and the list goes on.
    F. Shall I not seem to be needlessly drowning your ears
       by the number of their names?
       1. But the lands they dwelt in and their very tombs
          prove that they were human beings.
    G. As for the Muses, these were Mysian serving-maids
       purchased by Megaclo, the daughter of Macar (the
       king of the Lesbians). The account of them is found
       in Myrsilus of Lesbos.

XII. Now listen to the loves of these gods of yours and to
the extraordinary tales of their incontinence.
A. Call Poseidon, and the band of maidens corrupted by
him.
1. Yet, in spite of this great number of maidens, the
passions of your Poseidon were still unsatisfied.
B. Above all, let Zeus come too, who was so completely given over to lust that every woman not only ex-
cited his desire, but became a victim of it.
C. Heracles is the son of Zeus and a true son he is; for
in a single night he corrupted the fifty daughters of
Thestius, becoming at once bridegroom and adulter-
er to all these maidens.
D. Your gods did not abstain even from boys!
E. Let these be they (the gods) whom your boys are
trained to reverence, in order that they may grow to
manhood with the gods ever before them as a mani-
fest pattern of fornication.
F. But perhaps in the case of the gods, it is the males
only who rush eagerly after sexual delights, because
the goddesses are taken in modesty .
1. Yet, these are more passionately given to licentiousness, being fast bound in adultery, e.g., Eos
with Tithonus, etc.

XIII. Let us now proceed briefly to review the contests, and
let us put an end to these solemn assemblages at the
tombs: for these games are held in honor of the dead.
A. Now it seems that the contests, being held in honor
of the dead, were of the nature of mysteries, just as
also the oracles were; and both have become public
institutions.
B. But the contests are now a world-wide disgrace, as
are also the phalloi consecrated to Dionysus, from
the infection which they have spread over human
life.
C. This is the origin of these phalloi.
1. Dionysus, wishing to descend to Hades, asks the
man Prosymnus for directions.

2. Prosymnus gives the directions, but only after an obscene promise of reward is coaxed out of a willing Dionysus.
3. Upon his return Dionysus seeks Prosymnus, to fulfill the promise, only to find him dead.
4. At a mystic memorial of his passion phalloi are set up to Dionysus in cities, not so much for the sake of bodily intoxication as for licentiousness.

XIV. It would seem natural, therefore, for gods like these of yours to be slaves, since they have become slaves of their passions.
   A. Apollo bowed beneath the yoke of slavery to Admetus, and Heracles to Omphale.
      1. Other examples of such slavery revealed.
   B. As a natural consequence, these amorous and passionate gods of yours are brought before us as subject to every sort of human emotion.
      1. "For mortal flesh is theirs," and Homer gives evidence of this when he tells us of how Aphrodite uttered a loud cry over her wound.
   C. It is necessary, therefore, to supply the gods with attendance and nourishment, of which they are in need; if they were immortal, and in need of nothing, they would not partake of human pleasures.
      1. Zeus himself shared a human table among the Ethiopians, and he glutted himself with human flesh.
      2. What a fine Zeus he is, the diviner, the protector of guests, the hearer of suppliants: rather he ought to be called the unjust, the unrestrained.
      3. Still, there was life about him in those days, when he was a man; but now these legends have grown old.
      4. Where is Zeus himself: He has grown old, wings and all.
      5. See, the legend is laid bare. Zeus is dead (but, take it not to heart)!

XV. But it is clear that even the daemon-worshipers themselves are coming to understand the error about their
gods.
   A. The gods are of the race of men, though very shortly
they will be found to be nothing but oaks and rocks.
(sundry examples adduced)
   B. Do you think that the examples which I am adducing
are brought to you from some improper source?
      1. Why, it seems as if you do not recognize your
own authors, whom I call as witnesses against your
unbelief.
   C. Alas for you! They have filled your whole life with
godless foolery, until life has become truly intolera-
ble.
   D. Such is the character of the Greek gods; such, too,
are the worshipers, who make a mockery of the divine and of themselves.
   E. Now much better are Egyptians, when in cities and
villages they hold in great honor the irrational ani-
mals than Greeks who worship gods such as these?
      1. Though the Egyptians' gods are beasts, still they
are not adulterous.

XVI. Since they whom you serve are not gods, I am re-
solved to make a fresh examination to see whether it
is true that they are daemons, and should be enrolled
in the second rank of divinities. (further examples adduced.)
   A. Perhaps these ones guard us so that we might not
run away, or perhaps it is to keep us from sinning.
   B. Yet, if they really are guardians, they are not moved
by feelings of good will towards us.
      1. They seem more intent upon your destruction.
   C. Such is the character of the daemons and gods you
worship, for you have no poverty—not even of
words to form into the compounds needed for your
impiety.

(N.B.   To understand the point of Clement's onslaught

against the "daemons" it must be remembered that the best Greek teachers of his age used the doctrine of "secondary divinities" as a means of preserving their own monotheism without altogether breaking away from the popular mythology. According to them the one Supreme God worked through many ministers, to whom worship could rightly be offered. Clement attacks this position from the moral standpoint; the legends and the animal sacrifices prove that all these divinities, whether called gods, demigods, or anything else, were evil in character; there was no distinction between Zeus and the humblest daemon.)

Chapter Three: The Cruelty of the Sacrifices to the Gods

I. Come then, your gods are inhuman and man-hating daemons, who not only exult over the insanity of men, but go so far as to enjoy human slaughter.
   A. They provide pleasure for themselves by armed contests in the stadium and by wars, to gain their fill of human blood.
   B. They have fallen like plagues on cities and nations and demanded savage oblations.
      1. For instance, Aristomenes the Messenian sacrificed three hundred men to Zeus to gain favorable omens.
      2. The Taurians sacrifice strangers in their territory to Artemis.
   C. The daemons are kindly beings, as these instances show.
   D. And how can the worshipers of these daemons help but be holy in a corresponding manner?
      1. The daemons are called by the name savior: the worshipers beg for safety from these very saviors.
   E. They imagine that they sacrifice with good omens to them, and forget that they themselves are slaughtering men.
      1. Murder does not become a sacred offering be-

cause of the place in which it is committed.
2. On the contrary, such sacrifice is murder and human butchery.
F. Why is it, O men, that we fly from savage wild beasts, yet when faced by deadly and accursed daemons, you do not turn aside nor avoid them?

II. I can at once prove to you that man is better than these gods of yours, the daemons.
A. Your Phoebus is a lover of gifts but not of men.
1. He betrayed his friend Croesus, and led the king across the river Halys to his funeral pyre.
B. Do thou, Solon, utter an oracle of truth. Mark! it is not the daemon, but the man who tells thee the issue of life.
1. Unlike Apollo, Solon utters no double-meaning prophecies.

III. I cannot help wondering, therefore, what delusive fancies could have led astray those who were the first to be themselves deceived: such men as the well-known Phoroneus, or Merops.
A. There can be no doubt that in succeeding ages men used to invent gods whom they might worship.
1. This Eros, for instance, who is said to be among the oldest of the gods, was not honored before Charmus carried off a young lad.
2. Nor did the Athenians know who Pan was until Phillippidis told them.
B. We must not then be surprised that, once daemon-worship had begun, it became a fountain of insensate wickedness.
1. It ever increases and flows in full stream, establishes itself as creator of a multitude of daemons.
2. It sets up statues and builds temples, which are tombs in reality.
C. I appeal to you, even at this late hour, forget daemon-worship, feeling ashamed to honor tombs.

1. Unless a touch of shame steals over you for these audacities, then you are going about utterly dead, like the dead in whom you have put your trust.

Chapter Four: The Absurdity and Shamefulness of the Images by Which the Gods Are Worshiped

I. If I bring the statues and place them by your side for inspection, you will find on going through them that custom is truly nonsense, when it leads you to adore senseless things.

  A. The Scythians used to worship the dagger, the Arabians their sacred stone, other peoples still more ancient erected wooden poles and set up pillars of stones.

    1. When these rude images (called *xoana*) began to be shaped to the likeness of men, they acquired the additional name *brete*, meaning mortals.

    2. The moment art flourished, error increased.

  B. It is self-evident that out of matter men fashioned statues resembling the human form, to which you offer piety calumniating the truth.

  C. Still, since the point calls for a certain amount of argument, we must not decline to furnish it.

    1. Various and sundry examples of human construction of idols are given.

  D. But why do I linger over these, when I can show you the origin of the arch-daemon himself, whom they have dared to say is made without hands, the Egyptian Sarapis?

    1. Some relate that he was sent by the people of Sinope as a thankoffering to Ptolemy Philadelphus, king of Egypt.

    2. Others say that Sarapis was an image from Pontus, and that it was conveyed to Alexandria with the honor of a solemn festival.

    3. But Athenodorus, while intending to establish the antiquity of Sarapis, stumbled in some unac-

countable way, for he has proved him to be a statue made by man.*

*Sesostris the Egyptian king gave personal orders that a statue of Osiris should be elaborately wrought; and the statue was made by Bryasis, who has used a mixture of various materials in its construction.

II. Another fresh divinity was created in Egypt when the Roman king solemnly elevated to the rank of God his favorite whose beauty was unequalled.
   A. He consecrated Antinous in the same way that Zeus consecrated Ganymedes.
      1. For lust is not easily constrained, when it has no fear.
   B. Become a king over beauty, not a tyrant. Let it remain free.
      1. When you have kept its image pure, then I will acknowledge your beauty. Then I will worship beauty.
   C. But now we have a tomb of the boy who was loved, a temple and a city of Antinous: and it seems to me that tombs are objects of reverence in just the same way as temples are.
   D. Sybil calls the temple ruins.
      1. Hear Heraclitus of Ephesus, when he taunts the statues for their want of feeling.
   E. For are they not to be wondered at who worship stones, and place them before the doors, as if capable of activity.
      1. For if people upbraid them with being devoid of sensation, why worship them as gods? And, if they are thought to be endowed with sensation, why place them before the door?

III. But senseless wood and stone, and rich gold, care not a whit for either savoury odor, or blood, or smoke, by which, being at once honored and fumigated, they are blackened.

   A. These images are more worthless than any animal.
   B. For even though there are some living creatures
      which do not possess all the senses, yet these are
      better than those images and statues which are en-
      tirely dumb. For they have at any rate some one
      sense.
      1. The statues are motionless things incapable of ac-
         tion or sensation.
      2. The dumb earth is dishonored when sculptors by
         their art entice men to worship it.
   C. The god-makers worship not gods and daemons, but
      earth and art, which is all the statues are.
   D. In our view the image of God is not an object of
      sense but a mental object.
      1. The only true God is perceived not by the senses
         but by the mind.

IV. And again, when involved in calamities, the supersti-
    tious worshipers of stones, though they have learned by
    the event that senseless matter is not to be worshiped,
    yet they become victims of their superstition.
   A. Their folly is exposed by the impotence of the very
      gods to whom the statues are dedicated.
   B. Indeed, tyrants often plunder the riches of these stat-
      ues and are not punished.
      1. Swallows and most other birds settle on these
      very statues and defile them.
      2. And even their example does not bring home to
      you the absurdity of what you do.
   C. But it has also happened that miscreants or enemies
      have assailed and set fire to temples, and plundered
      them of their votive gifts from base greed of gain.
   D. If such villany proves nothing, then let us look at fire
      and earthquakes.
      1. They are in no way intent on gain, yet they are
      not frightened by the daemons any more than are
      the waves by the pebbles strewn along the shore.
   E. If you wish to cease from your folly, the fire shall be
      your guiding.

       1. The temple of Argos and others have been de-
voured by fire.
  F. Here you see a kind of prelude to what the fire promises to do hereafter.

V. And the makers of images, do they not shame those of
you who are wise into despising matter.
  A. Praxiteles, when fashioning the statue of Cnidian
Aphrodite, made the goddess resemble his mistress,
that the people might worship his mistress.
    1. It remains for you to judge if you wish to extend
your worship to courtesans.
  B. Such were the facts that moved the kings of old, in
their contempt for these legends to proclaim themselves gods.
    1. In this way they teach us that the other gods were
also men, made immortal by their renown.
  C. And not kings only, but private persons dignified
themselves with the names of deities.
  D. Indeed whole nations and cities belittle the legends
about the gods by transforming men like themselves
into the equals of the gods and voting them extrava-
gant honors.
  E. This is the oracle of Hippo; let us understand its
meaning. Those whom you worship were once men,
who afterwards died.
    1. Legend and the lapse of time have given them
their honors.
    2. For what is present is despised through familiari-
ty: the past being separated from immediate ex-
posure by the obscurtiy which time brings, is in-
vested with a fictitious honor.
    3. Therefore, while the events of the present are dis-
trusted, those of the past are regarded with rev-
erent wonder.
  F. As an example, the dead men of old are believed to
be gods by those who come after.

VI. You are right then in having yourselves called the gods

"shadows" and "daemons."
A. For Homer spoke of Athena and her fellow-deities as
   "daemons," paying them a malicious compliment.
   (*Iliad* i. 221-222)
B. How then can the shadows and daemons any longer
   be gods, when they are in reality unclean and loath-
   some spirits.
C. Such things are your gods—shades and shadows
   (shadows and daemons), and to these add those
   maimed, wrinkled, squinting divinities the Litae.
D. Alas for such atheism! You sink in the earth the incorruptible existence and that which is stainless and
   holy you have buried in the tombs.
   1. Thus, you have robbed the divine of its real and
      true being.

VII. Why have you forsaken heaven to pay honor to earth?
     For what else is gold, or silver, or other metals? Are
     they not earth and made from earth?
     A. Why then did you blaspheme highest heaven and
        drag down piety to the ground by fashioning for
        yourselves gods of earth?
     B. Why have you fallen into deeper darkness by going
        after these created things instead of the uncreated
        God?

VIII. The ivory is beautiful, but matter will ever be in need
      of art, but God has no such need.
      A. Art develops, matter is invested with shape; the cost-
         liness of the substance makes it worth carrying off
         for gain, but it is the shape alone which makes it an
         object of veneration.
      B. But my practice is to walk upon earth, not to worship
         it. For I hold it wrong to entrust my spirit's hopes to
         things
      C. Therefore, we must inspect the statues most carefully
         to prove that they are inseparably associated with
         error.

      1. For their forms are unmistakably stamped with the marks of the daemons.

      2. If one were to go round inspecting the paintings and statues, he would recognize your gods from their shameful forms.

   D. Such strength had art to beguile so that it became for amorous men a guide to the pit of destruction.

   E. How craftsmanship is powerful, but it cannot beguile a rational being.

      1. It is true that a maiden once fell in love with an image, but it was her sight that was beguiled by the art.

      2. For no man in his senses would have embraced the statue of a goddess .

IX. But in your case art has another illusion with which to beguile, for it leads you on to honor and worship them.

   A. The painting, you say, is lifelike. Let the art be praised, but let it not beguile man by pretending to be truth.

   B. Such insane passion did the arts implant in creatures without sense.

   C. Even monkeys know better than this.

      1. But you will prove yourselves inferior even to monkeys through the heed you pay to statues.

   D. Such are the pernicious playthings made for you by the artists.

   1. Even magicians boast that the gods are their thralls, assisting them in their evil incantations.

X. Further, the marriages of gods and their acts of lechery, debauchery, and drunkenness, exhort me to cry aloud!

   A. Under the masks of daemons you have made comedy of that which is holy.

   B. Cease the song, Homer (*Odyssey* viii, 267-270). There is no beauty in that; it teaches adultery.

   C. We have declined to lend even our ears to fornication. For we are they who bear about the image of

God, an image which dwells in us, which is our
counsellor and companion.
1. We have been made a consecrated offering to
God for Christ's sake.
2. We are they who are not "from below," but have
learnt the whole truth from Him who came from
above (John 3:31).

XI. But most men are not of this mind. They have their
homes decorated with pictures depicting the unnatural
lust of the daemons.
A. These are the patterns for your voluptuousness; these
are the lessons taught by gods who are fornicators
like yourselves.
B. You behold without a blush the postures of such li-
centious art displayed in public.
1. But when they are hung in your houses you treasure them still more, as if they were actually the
images of your gods.
C. We declare that not only their use, but also the sight
of these things should be forgotten.
D. You who have done violence to man and erased the
divine image in which he was created, you are utter
unbelievers in order that you may give way to your
passions.
E. You disbelieve in God because you cannot bear self-
control.

XII. The only men who can be called "blessed" are those
whom Sybil describes "Who, seeing the temples, will
reject them all." (*Oracles* iv. 24, 27-30)
A. What is more, we are expressly forbidden to practice
a deceitful art (Ex 20:4)
B. But as for you, you never give a thought to prevent
yourselves turning out like statues owing to want of
sense.
C. The prophetic word refutes the custom of idolatry
when it says, "All the gods of the nations are images

of daemons; but God made the heavens." (Ps 96:5)
1. Some, it is true, go astray and worship not God
   but his handiwork absurdly supposing these to
   be gods.
D. But while human handiwork fashions artifices how
   can I speak of all that God creates?
   1. See the whole universe, that is His work.
E. How great is the power of God! His mere will is
   creation; for God alone created, since he alone is
   truly God.
   1. By a bare wish His work is done, and the world's
      existence follows upon a single act of His will.
F. Let none of you worship the sun; rather let him yearn
   for the maker of the sun.
G. It seems that but one refuge remains for the man
   who is to reach the gates of salvation, and that is divine wisdom.
   1. From thence no longer can any daemon carry him
      off, as he presses onward to salvation.

**Chapter Five: The Opinions of the Philosophers
                  Respecting God***

I. Let us now run through the opinions which the philoso-
   phers assert about the Gods.
   A. We may find philosophy herself forming her con-
      ceptions of the godhead out of matter.
      1. Or, when deifying certain divine powers, she sees
         the truth in a dream.
   B. Some philosophers left us the elements as first prin-
      ciples of all things.
      1. Water was selected by Thales.
      2. Air by Anaximes.

*Cf. Hippolytus, *Against All Heresies,* who traces all the
early heresies back to particular Greek philosophical
schools.

    3. Fire and earth by Parmenides.
C. These men were really atheists, since they worshiped
    matter.
    1. Although they did not worship statues they wor-
       shiped earth the mother of these.
    2. They do not fashion a Poseidon, but they adore
       water itself.
D. The followers of Heraclitus worship fire as the
    source of all.
    1. The Persian Magi have assigned honor to fire.
    2. Dino says that these Magi sacrifice under the
       open sky, believing that fire and water are the
       sole emblems of divinity.

II. Even their ignorance I do not conceal: they are quite
    convinced that they are escaping idolatry, yet they slip
    into another delusion.
A. They do not suppose, like Greeks, that stocks and
    stones are emblems of divinity, but they admit fire
    and water, as the philosophers do.
B. It was not till many ages had passed that they began
    to worship statues in human form.
    1. This custom was introduced by Artaxerxes.
C. Let the philosophers therefore confess who their
    teachers are from whom they have learnt the atheis-
    tic doctrine of "first principles."
D. The creator of the "first principles" themselves, God
    without beginning, they do not know, but offer ado-
    ration to these "weak and beggarly elements." (Gal
    4:9)

III. Other philosophers went beyond the elements and
    sought for a more excellent principle.
A. Some praised the Infinite, as did Anaximander,
    Anaxagoras, and Archelaus.
    1. The two latter, however, agreed in placing Mind
       above the Infinite while others held as first prin-
       ciples "fulness" and "void."
B. Nor was this all, Alcmaeon thought that the stars

were endowed with life and therefore gods.
C. The Stoics say that the divine nature permeated all matter, even in its lowest forms.
   1. These men simply cover philosophy with shame.
D. The father of the Peripatetics, Aristotle, did not perceive the Father of all things, but thought that he who is called the "Highest" is the soul of the universe.
   1. But he supposes the soul of the world to be God, so he is pierced by his own sword.
E. Epicurus alone I will banish from memory for he thinks that God has no care for the world.

Chapter Six: By Divine Inspiration Philosophers Sometimes Hit on the Truth*

I. And a vast crowd of the same description swarms upon me, bringing in their train an absurd picture of strange daemons.
A. Far indeed are we from allowing grown men to listen to such tales.
   1. Even to our own children, we are not in the habit of telling fabulous stories.
   2. We shrink from fostering in the children the atheism proclaimed by these men, who have no more knowledge of the truth than infants .
B. Why do you infect life with idols, imagining winds, air, fire, etc., to be gods ?
C. I long for the Lord of the winds, the Lord of fire, the Creator of the world; He who gives light to the sun.
D. Whom shall I take as a helper in my inquiry? We do not wholly disown Plato.
   1. Passages taken from *Timaeus* (28 c.) describe the incomprehensibility of God.

*A Philonic theory.

2. Well done, Plato, you have hit the truth. But do
   not give up.

II. For there is a certain divine effluence instilled into all
    men without exception, wherefore they admit, even
    though against their will, that God is One.
    A. Menander describes God as the essence of the Sun.
    B. But not even the sun could ever show us the true
       God.
       1. The healthful Word, that is the Sun of the soul,
          alone can do that, through him alone the soul's
          eye is illuminated.
    C. Plato says darkly (Epistles ii), "All things are around
       the king of all things and that is the cause of every-
       thing good."
    D. Who, then is the king of all things? It is God, the
       measure of the truth of all existence.
       1. As things measured are comprehended by the
          measure, so also by the perception of God is the
          truth measured and comprehended.
       2. God is the weight and measure and number of the
          universe
       3. The one true God, who is the only just measure,
          measures and weighs all things, encircling and
          sustaining the nature of the universe by His jus-
          tice.
    E. Whence, Plato, do you hint at the truth?
       1. I know your teachers and the sources of your wis-
          dom; but as for your laws and your belief about
          God, you have been helped by the Hebrews
          themselves.

III. And now, O philosophy, hasten to set before me not
     only this one man Plato, but many others also, who de-
     clare the one only true God to be God.
     A. Antisthenes had perceived this and Xenophon.
     B. Cleanthes of Pisadeus sets forth no genealogy of the
        gods, rather he sets forth a true theology.
        1. He teaches clearly what is the nature of God, and

how common opinion and custom make slaves
of those who follow them instead of searching
after God.
C. These sayings have been recorded by their authors
through God's inspiration .
1. As a guide to the full knowledge of God they are
sufficient for every man who is able to in-
vestigate the truth.

Chapter Seven: The Poets also Bear Testimony to the
Truth

I. But we will not rest content with philosophy alone. Let
poetry also approach to bear witness to truth, or rather to
confess before God its deviation into fable.
A. Aratus perceives that the power of God permeates
the universe.
B. Euripides and Sophocles unveil the truth upon the
stage.
C. And the Thracian, Orpheus, brings in a recantation
consisting of truth.

II. It may be freely granted that the Greeks received some
glimmerings of the divine word, and gave utterance to a
few scraps of truth.
A. On the other hand, they convict themselves of weak-
ness, since they failed to reach the end.
B. It is plain to all that those who do anything or utter
anything without the word of truth are like men
struggling to walk without a foothold.

III. The comic poets also bring into their plays convincing
arguments against your gods.
A. Let these shame you into salvation.
1. Menander and Antisthenes ridicule the gods.
2. Not only these, but also Homer, Euripides, and
many other poets expose your gods.
B. Euripides is indeed a worthy disciple of the Socratic

school, in that he regarded only the truth and disregarded the audience.

Chapter Eight: The True Doctrine Is To Be Sought in the Prophets

I. It is time to turn to the writings of the prophets. For these are the oracles which lay a firm foundation for the truth.
  A. The sacred writings are also modes of virtuous living, and short roads to salvation.
    1. They are bare of embellishment, yet they raise up man when fast bound in the grip of evil.
  B. They provide a cure for many ills, and urge us onward with clear guidance to salvation set before our eyes.
  C. Let the Prophetess, the Sibyl, first sing to us the song of salvation.
    1. With true inspiration she likens delusion to darkness, and the knowledge of God to the sun and light: she teaches what our choice should be.

II. Now Jeremiah, or rather the Holy Spirit in Jeremiah, shows what God is. "I am," he says, "a God who is near, and not a God afar off." (Jer 23: 23-24) .
  A The same Spirit speaks through Isaiah of God's greatness. (Is 40:12)
  B. He is God, the prophet Isaiah says again, "whose throne is heaven, and the earth His footstool." (Is 64:1 in the Septuagint)
  C. Would you hear too, what this prophet says about idol-worshipers and how they will be destroyed? (Jer 8:2; 34:20; etc.)
    1. He says that the elements and the world shall be destroyed with them.

III. But will you listen to yet another giver of oracles? What says the Holy Spirit to them through Hosea and Isaiah?
  A. Are you then still idol-worshipers? Yet, even now

beware of God's threats.
1. For the carved images shall cry out, or rather they who trust in them; for the material is incapable of feeling.
B. Why tell you of mysteries of wisdom, and of sayings that come from a Hebrew child who was endowed with wisdom?
1. The Word of the Father, the good lamp, the Lord who brings light, faith, and salvation to all will come to you.
2. When we have fallen to idols, wisdom, which is His Word, restores us to truth.

IV. This is the first resurrection, the resurrection from transgression; wherefore Moses, turning us away from all idolatry, exclaims, "Hear O Israel, the Lord is thy God, the Lord is one." (Dt 6:4)
A. And, in His great pity for us, the Lord raises high the strain of salvation.
B. Why do you love vanity and seek after falsehood? What, then, is this vanity and falsehood?
1. The apostle of the Lord explains it when he says that the Greeks knew God and yet did not glorify him, choosing an image instead. (Rom 1:21-ff)
C. Yet, you do not perceive God, but worship the heaven. How can you escape the charge of impiety?

Chapter Nine: "That Those Grievously Sin Who Despise Or Neglect God's Gracious Calling."

I. I could adduce ten thousand Scriptures of which not "one tittle shall pass away" without being fulfilled.
A. He speaks not as a teacher to disciples, nor as a master to servants, nor as God to men, but as a "tender father" admonishing his sons.
1. Thus, Moses confesses that "he was filled with quaking and terror" while he listened to God

speaking concerning the Word.
B. Are you not afraid when you listen to the divine
   Word Himself? Are you not troubled? Are you not
   eager for salvation, fearing God's wrath, loving His
   grace, striving after the hope, in order that you may
   escape the judgment?
C. We must become as children to receive the Father.
   1. A stranger is enrolled and made a citizen when he
      becomes as a child and receives the Father, then
      he will share the Father's kingdom with the true
      Son.
   2. This is the "church of the firstborn," which is
      composed of many good children.
   3. And we are these first-born sons, we who are
      God's nurslings, the first to be separated from
      the devil.

II. Yet the truth is, that the more God loves them the more
    do some men depart from Him.
    A. God wishes us to become sons, but they have
       disdained even to become sons. What folly!
       1. He promises freedom, but you run away into
          slavery.
       2. The apostle repudiates such behavior. (Eph 4:17-
          19)
    B. After the accusation of such a witness what else re-
       mains for the unbelieving than judgment and con-
       demnation.
       1. Yet, the Lord does not weary of admonishing,
          warning, and calling.
       2. He awakens men from sleep, and those that have
          gone astray He causes to rise from out of the
          darkness itself.
    C. Let no one then despise the Word, lest he unwitting-
       ly despise himself.
    D. For great is the grace of His promise, "if to-day we
       hear his voice."
       1. And this "to-day" is extended day by day as long
          as the word "to-day" exists.

2. Both the "to-day" and the teaching continue until the consummation of all things, and then the true "to-day" begins for all ages.

E. For "to-day" is an image of the everlasting age, and the day is a symbol of light, and the light of men is the Word, through whom we gaze upon God.

F. Naturally, then, grace will abound towards those who have believed and listen; but as for those who have disbelieved and are erring in heart, with them God is displeased, and them He threatens.

   1. Indeed the ancient Hebrews received in a figure the fulfillment of the threat when they wandered in the desert.

III. But the Lord, in His love for man, invites all men to the knowledge of the truth, and for this end sends the Paraclete. This knowledge is godliness .

A. If eternal salvation were for sale, how much would you pay for it?

   1. Truly no price can buy it.

B. But do not despair. It is in your power to buy this salvation with a treasure of your own, faith and love.

   1. This price God is pleased to accept.

IV. But Godliness designates God as our suitable teacher, who alone can worthily assimilate man to God.

A. For the letters which make us sacred are themselves sacred, and thus the Scriptures.

B. No one could be so deeply moved at the exhortations of other holy men as those of the Lord, for this is His only work that man be saved.

   1. He converts men when they come to him in fear.

C. But you have so little fear, or rather faith, that you obey neither the Lord nor Paul, His servant.

D. Faith shall lead you, the Scripture shall train you.

E. We are they, the worshipers of the good, who are zealous for good things.

F. The Word was not hidden from any; He is a univer-

sal light; He shines on all men.
1. Let us hasten to salvation and the new birth.
2. Let us be gathered into one love corresponding to
    the union of the One Being.
3. Let us follow after unity by the practice of good
    works, seeking the good Monad.
G. This is the true speech which God welcomes from
    His children. This is the first-fruits of God's harvest.

Chapter Ten: Answer to the Objection of the Heathen,
                 That It Was Not Right To Abandon the Cus-
                 toms of Their Fathers

I. But, you say, it is not reasonable to overthrow a way of
   life handed down to us from our forefathers.
   A. If this is the case then why do we not continue to use
      our first food, milk, to which our nurses accustomed
      us from birth?
      1. Again, deviations in course at sea are dangerous,
         but are attended by a certain charm.
   B. In life itself shall we not abandon the old way, which
      is wicked and without God?
      1. Shall we not bend our course towards the truth
         and seek after our real Father, thrusting away
         custom as some deadly thing?
   C. It was from madness and from this thrice miserable
      custom that hatred of godliness sprang.
      1. For a boon so great, the greatest ever given by
         God to the human race, would never have been
         hated and rejected, had not you been carried
         away by custom.
   D. You yearned to shake yourselves free from us, the
      charioteers of your life and supposed the holy Word
      of God to be accursed.
   E. You do not know that this is true above all else, that
      the good and god-fearing shall meet with a reward
      that is good, while the wicked shall meet with pun-
      ishment corresponding to their deeds.

F. God grants life; but wicked custom inflicts unavail-
   ing repentance together with punishment when we
   depart from this world.

II. Let any of you look at those who minister before the
    idols, their persons filthy and unkempt, and many of
    them castrated: these men seem to mourn for the gods,
    not to worship them.
   A. Now God is a Father and seeks his creatures.
      1. Dogs who have lost their way discover their
         master's tracks by the sense of smell.
   B. But you are lost and do not know Him. What
      then does the Lord do? He bears no grudge; He still
      pities, still requires repentance of us.
   C. How can you live such lives! There are some who
      wallow in marshes and mud, which are the streams
      of pleasure, and feed on profitless and senseless de-
      lights.
   D. As true "children of the light" let us direct our gaze
      steadily upward towards the light.
      1. Let us therefore repent, and pass from ignorance
         to knowledge.
   E. It is a glorious venture to desert to God's side. Many
      are the good things which we may enioy who are
      lovers of righteousness.
   F. Aye, and a glorious and lovely inheritance is that
      treasure of salvation, towards which we must press
      forward by becoming lovers of the Word.

III. This inheritance is entrusted to us by the eternal cove-
     nant of God, which supplies the eternal gift.
   A. It is to the font, to salvation, to enlightenment that
      He invites us.
   B. The truth is not sold as merchandise. The bastard,
      who has chosen to "serve mammon," shall buy them
      (the things of the earth) with money; but to you, to
      the true son, He gives what is your own.
   C. The saints of the Lord shall inherit God's glory and
      power. What kind of glory? A glory "which eye

hath not seen, nor ear heard, nor hath it entered into
the heart of man." (1 Cor 2:9)

IV. Would you have me become a good counsellor to you?
Then listen, and I will show myself to be one.
   A. When reflecting upon the good itself, you ought to
      have called to your aid faith and with the utmost
      clearness to choose what is best.
   B. You fly into folly with reckless abandon and without
      question, but it would seem when godliness is in
      question, you first inquire; and when it is a question
      of following God you deliberate and reflect, when
      you have no idea of what is worthy of God.
      1. Put your faith in us, even as you do in riotous in-
         dulgence, that you may live.
      2. Let no feeling of shame for the name of Christian
         deter you, for shame harms when it turns you
         aside from salvation.

V. Having then stripped before the eyes of all, let us join in
   the real contest in the arena, where the Word is umpire
   and the Master is president.
   A. For the prize set before us is no small one, immor-
      tality.
   B. Cease then to pay any further heed to the speeches
      made to you by the rabble.
      1. For these are they who have dared to deify men.
   C. Indeed, he who worships gods that are visible and at-
      taches himself to them, is a far more wretched ob-
      ject than the very demons.
   D. For God is righteous in the highest possible degree,
      and there is nothing more like Him than one of us
      who becomes as righteous as possible.
      1. For "the image of God" is His word and an image
         of the Word is the true man, that is, the mind of
         man, who on this account is said to have been
         created "in the image" of God, and "in His like-
         ness," because through his understanding heart

he is made like the divine Word and so reasonable

E. Nothing else but madness has taken possession of life, when it spends itself with so much earnestness upon matter.
  1. Custom, has been fostered by idle opinion.
  2. It is ignorance that brought mankind to the brink of destruction and idolatry.
F. Receive then the water of reason. Be washed, you that are defiled by custom.
  1 We must be pure to ascend to heaven.
  2. See your Father! For you are His son.
G. To whom shall the Lord say; "Yours is the kingdom of heaven?" It is yours, if you are willing simply to trust and follow the short way of our preaching.
H. How, then, may I ascend to heaven, is it said?
  1. The Lord is the way: a strait and narrow way to and from heaven.
  2. A way narrow and despised on earth, but broad and adored in heaven.

VI. He who has never heard the Word can plead ignorance as an excuse for his error, but the one who hears and disobeys, that one nurses his disobedience in his soul.
A. For it is his nature, as man, to be in close fellowship with God.
  1. We call upon man, who was made for the contemplation of heaven, to come to the knowledge of God.
  2. Having laid hold of what is personal in his nature, we counsel him to equip himself with godliness for his journey through eternity.

VII. Look about you and consider a little what is the meaning of your worship of stones.
A. You are wasting your life upon death.
B. Enslaved to pernicious custom, you cling to it of your own free will until the latest breath, and sink down into destruction.

C. Who, in his right mind, would imagine such things
   as correction, punishment, justice, and retribu-
   tion to be God's?
   1. If you deify modesty, desire and love, you must
     add to them shame, impulse, beauty, and sexual
     intercourse.
D. If we do not believe even one of these to be a god,
   then nothing remains except to confess that the only
   true God is the one who is and subsists.

VIII. But those who are insensible to this are like men who
    have drunk mandrake. May God grant that you may at
    length awake from this slumber and know God.
   A. It is written that "the earth is the Lord's." How is it
     then that you enjoy its fruits while ignoring its Mas-
     ter?
   B. Acknowledge your Master. You are God's own
     handiwork.
    1. For what is alienated, being deprived of its con-
      nection with Him, is deprived of the truth.
   C. Believe that these things are being spoken to you
     from heaven.
    1. Regard men as really sacred and take beasts and
      stones for what they are.

IX. But He whose love for man is unspeakably great has
    also an unbounded hatred for sin.
   A. His wrath breeds the punishment to follow upon: His
     love for man brings blessings upon repentance.
   B. The blinding of the eyes and deafening of the ears
     are more grievous than all the encroachments of the
     evil one.
    1. By the first, we are robbed of the sight of heaven.
    2. By the second, we are deprived of the divine
      teaching.
   C. But nothing stands in the way of him who earnestly
     desires to come to the knowledge of God.
    1. For he who is zealous for the right is himself in

need of little, because he has stored up his bless-
edness with none other than God Himself.
D. Listen to me, and do not stop up your ears or shut off
your hearing, but consider my words.
1. Let us repent with our whole heart, that with our
whole heart we may be able to receive God.
2. Trust and take salvation for reward.
E. He who seeks after God is busy about his own salvation.
1. The reward of finding is life with God.
F. A beautiful hymn to God is an immortal man who is
being built up in righteousness, and upon whom the
oracles of truth have been engraved.
1. The wisdom of the righteous man, found in the
Father, leads to excellence in all stations of life.

X. Surely the beasts are happier than men who live in error!
They dwell in error, like you, but do not pretend to
know the truth.
A. When you think of this are you not ashamed that you
are less reasonable than the unreasonable creatures,
because you are atheists?
B. If you have respect for old age, be wise, now that
you have reached life's sunset, acquire the knowledge of God, that the end of life may prove to be the
beginning of salvation.
1. God will enroll you as guileless children.
C. But you are not able to endure the austerity of salvation.
1. Custom pleases us, but thrusts us into the pit,
whereas truth leads us up to heaven.
D. And be not afraid lest the multitude of pleasing objects which rise before you withdraw you from wisdom; of your own accord you will willingly pass beyond childishness of custom.
1. For not without divine care could so great a work
have been accomplished.
E. Through Christ's teachings and signs He showed
whence He came and who He was, namely, the

Word our herald, a spring of life and peace flooding the earth.

Chapter Eleven: How Great Are the Benefits Conferred on Man Through The Advent of Christ.

I. Now consider briefly the beneficence of God from the beginning.
   A. The first man played in Paradise with childlike freedom, since he was a child of God.
      1. But when he fell a victim to pleasure, the child was ashamed to meet God.
      2. The man who by reason of innocence had been free was discovered to be bound by sins.
   B. The Lord purposed to loose him from his bonds. Clothing Himself with bonds of flesh, He subdued the serpent and enslaved the tyrant death.
      1. The very man who had erred through pleasure was shown to be free again, through His outstretched hands.
      2. He who was driven from Paradise gains a greater prize, heaven, on becoming obedient.
   C. Since the Word Himself came to us from heaven, we ought no longer to go to human teaching.
      1. You will not disbelieve that we have entered into the really true wisdom which philosophers only hinted at, but which Christ's disciples have understood and proclaimed.

II, The exhortation that alone would seem to be universal and concerned with the whole of existence is piety towards God.
   A. It is only necessary to live according to piety in order to obtain eternal life.
   B. Let us admit the light, that we may admit God. Let us admit the light, and become disciples of the Lord.
   C. Away with our forgetfulness of the truth! Let us re-

move the ignorance and darkness so that we may
see God and praise His Light.
1. Upon us who lay buried in darkness a light shone
from heaven.
2. That light is life eternal, it gives life to all who
partake of it.
  D. The universe has become sleepless light and the setting has turned into a rising.
1. He it was who changed the setting into a rising,
and crucified death into life.

III. At the price of a little faith He gives you this great earth
to peruse for your benefit.
  A. All the works of creation He has given to you in return for a little faith.
  B. Put on the heavenly amulet, the Word who truly
saves, and be freed from the sins of the passions.
For sin is eternal death.
  C. Let the light shine in the hidden part of man, his
heart, and let it illumine with rays of knowledge the
joint-heir of Christ.

IV. It is God's eternal purpose to save the flock of mankind.
For this reason He sent the good Shepherd.
  A. This is the preaching of righteousness: to the obedi-
ent, good news; to the disobedient, a means of judgment.
  B. It is better for man to become both imitator and servant of the highest of all beings.
  C. Divine love comes to men in this way, the spark of
nobility is kindled afresh in the soul by the Word
and is permitted to shine forth, and salvation runs in
tandem with it.
  D. The wish of Christ is that you have life.
1. He is the uncorrupt Word who brings about all
things.
  E. Labor is wisdom for the harvest of self-control, and
present yourself to God for his delight.
  F. Two things are necessary for the friend of Christ; he

must be worthy of the kingdom, and be found worthy of the kingdom.

Chapter Twelve: Exhortation To Abandon Their Old Errors and Listen To the Instructions of Christ

I. Let us then shun custom; let us shun it as some dangerous headland, or threatening Charybdis, or the Sirens of legend.
    A. Custom strangles man, it turns him away from truth.
    B. Sailor, a heavenly wind comes to your aid. Pass by pleasure.
       1. Bound to the wood of the cross you shall live freed from all corruption.
       2. Then you shall have the vision of my God, and shall be initiated in those holy mysteries.
    C. I will show you the Word, and the mysteries of the Word, expounding them after your own fashion.
    D. The mysteries of God's holy mountain are expounded to the reader.
       1. This is the mountain beloved of God, a mount of sobriety.
       2. There revel on it the daughters of God, the fair lambs who celebrate the holy rites of the Word, raising a sober choral dance.
       3. The righteous are the chorus; the music is a hymn of the King of the universe.

II. Christ, by whom the eyes of the blind see again, shines upon you more brightly than the sun.
    A. O truly sacred mysteries! O pure light! In the blaze of the torches I have a vision of heaven and of God.
       1. The Lord reveals the mysteries.
    B. If you will, be initiated also, and you shall dance around the only true God, the Word of God joining with us in our hymn of praise.
       1. This Jesus being eternal, one great high priest of

one God is also Father, prays for men and en-
courages men.
C. Come, for to you alone is offered the fruit of immortality.
D. Let us love Christ, the noble charioteer of men.
   1. Having yoked together the team of mankind, He
      shapes the course of His chariot for the goal of
      immortality.
   2. He drove at the first into Jerusalem, but now into
      heaven, a most noble spectacle for the Father,
      the eternal Son bringing victory.
E. The Word is our helper; let us have confidence in
Him, and let no longing ever come upon us so
strongly as the longing after the Word of truth Himself.

III. The philosophers consider that all the works of foolish
men are unholy and impious, and by describing ignorance itself as a form of madness they acknowledge that
the mass of men are nothing else but mad.
A. Holding fast the truth with all our might we must
follow God in soundness of mind, and consider all
things to be His.
   1. We must recognize that we are the noblest of His
      possessions and entrust ourselves to Him.
B. It is time for us to say and believe that when a god-
fearing man has been made by Christ "just and holy
with understanding," he also becomes already like
God.
   1. The entire life of men who have come to know
      Christ is good.
C. It may be that I have run on too long in pouring out
what I have received from God, as is natural when
one is inviting men to the greatest of good things—
salvation.
D. But with you still rests the final act, namely this, to
choose which is the more profitable, judgment or
grace.

Clement of Alexandria
Quis Dives Salvetur?

A comparison of the trans. of G. W. Butterworth, *Clement of Alexandria* with an English translation. Loeb Classical library (1919), and A. Cleveland Coxe, *Ante-Nicene Fathers* (rev. ed.) (1885).

I. Those who praise the rich in hope of a large return are flatterers and are really impious and insidious.
  A. Impious because they give God's prerogative to those wallowing in debauchery.
  B. Insidious because they delude the minds of the rich by their immoderate praises and cause them to become contemptuous of everything.
  C. It is a far kinder act if we work out salvation for the rich by every means.
    1. First, by asking this of God, who gladly gives such gifts to His children.
    2. Second, heal their souls with reason and lead them to the possession of truth.
  D. The possessor of truth is distinguished by good works and (thereby) wins eternal life.

II. Reasons why the rich despair of salvation.
  A. Some, hearing the Lord's saying (Mt. 19:24) in an offhand way, despair of ever attaining eternal life and cling solely to this present life.
  B. Others understand the true meaning of the saying but fail to prepare themselves because they make light of the works which bear on salvation.

C. In both cases the rich have learned of Christ's salvation and power.

III. Christians must show the rich that salvation is not impossible.
A. They must first, by means of Scripture, relieve them of their unfounded despair, and show that the inheritance of the Kingdom of heaven is not cut off from them.
B. Then, when they have learned this, instruct them how and through what means they may obtain the object of their hope.
C. But, as with athletes, it is necessary for the rich man to exert effort in attaining this prize.
1. The rich man is not barred from the outset, if he is willing to discipline himself.
2. He is to let reason (*Logos*) be his trainer and Christ be the master of the contest.
3. When the last trumpet sounds to end the race, he may exit this life a victor.

IV. May the Saviour grant us power to impart to the (rich) brethren salutary thoughts, first, with regard to the hope, and, second, with regard to the means of reaching it.
A. Christ gives freely to those who need, shakes off their despair.
B. For we must bear the actual words again which have continued to trouble us in the Gospels. (Mk. 10:17-34)

V. Since we are aware that the Saviour teaches nothing in a merely human way, we must not understand his words literally, but must search out the hidden meaning.
A. The simplified sayings of the Lord need more attention than His dark sayings.
B. Surely the simplified sayings should not be taken as they strike the careless ear, but with an effort of

mind (*nous*) to reach Christ's secret meaning.

VI. For our Lord and Saviour is pleased to be asked a question most appropriate to Him, in order that He may reveal the purpose of the Gospel, that is a gift to eternal life.
A. As God Christ knows beforehand what questions He will be asked and what answers will be given Him.
B. When He is called good, He uses this as his starting point, turning the disciple to God who is good, and alone dispenser of eternal life.
  1. Which the Son gives to us after receiving it from Him.

VII. We must therefore know the eternal God as both giver of eternal gifts and first and supreme and one and a good God.
A. We can get possession of God through knowledge and apprehension.
B. Ignorance of Him is death, but full knowledge of Him is alone life.

VIII. He therefore that aims at living the true life is bidden first to know Him (God the Father) and then to understand the Saviour's greatness next to Him, and the newness of His grace.
A. If the law of Moses was able to supply eternal life, it is in vain that the Saviour comes Himself to us and suffers on our account.
  1. In vain also is the rich man asking immortality from another.
B. Nevertheless the young man in question is positively convinced that life is lacking altogether to him.
  1. So He asks it from Him who alone is able to give it.
  2. He passes over "from faith to faith." (Rom. 1:17)

IX. Jesus loves the rich man yet calls him imperfect as regards eternal life, because he is idle in respect of true life.
   A. Now the works of the law are good but only to the extent of being a sort of training, leading one to the supreme law-giving and grace of Jesus Christ.
   B. However, Christ is the fulfillment of the law for all who believe (Rom. 10:4; 13:10)
      1. Christ does not make slaves but sons, brothers, and joint heirs.

X. The rich man was not yet perfect but the choice lay with the man as a free being, though the gift was with God as Lord. (*hos kuriō*)
   A. God does not compel, but He provides for those who seek. (Mt. 7:7)
   B. "The thing thou lackest," the one thing, that which is Mine, which is peculiar to those who live.
      1. The rich man went away displeased, for he did not truly wish for life.
      2. The work that brings life he was not able to accomplish.
   C. He bade this man cease from his manifold activities and cling to the grace of Him who adds eternal life.

XI. The meaning of the command—"Sell what belongs to you."
   A. It is not a command to fling away the substance that belongs to him, but to banish from the soul his opinions about riches.
   B. For it is no great or enviable thing to be simply without riches, apart from the purpose of obtaining life.
   C. Nor again is it a new thing to renounce wealth and give it freely to the poor.
      1. Such men as Anaxagoras, Democritus and Crates did it.

XII. The command does not refer to the visible act, but to stripping the soul and the will of all alien thoughts.
   A. The men of former days parted with their possessions, but they intensified the passions of their souls.
   B. A further point: It is possible, after unburdening oneself of one's property, to be continually absorbed in the desire for the support of riches.
   C. When a man lacks the necessities of life he will tend to be broken in spirit and to neglect the higher things.

XIII. For what snaring would be left among men, if nobody had anything?
   A. Conflicting passages commending the use of wealth adduced from Scripture.
      1. Make friends with unrighteous mammon. (Lk.16:9)
      2. Acquire treasure in heaven. (Mt. 6:20)
   B. The proper use of riches; that He commands them to be shared.
   C. It would be the height of unreason to believe that we are to stand aloof from riches while yet being commanded to share of them with others.

XIV. We must not fling away the riches that are of benefit to our neighbors as well as ourselves.
   A. Riches are put at our disposal as instruments to be well used by those who know (how to use them).
   B. So let a man do away with the passions of his soul, which do not consent to the better use of what he has.

XV. Two kinds of possessions: those within the soul and those without it.
   A. Those without are good or bad only in relation to the soul's use of them.
   B. What does Christ command us to rid ourselves of?
      1. A man must say good-bye to the injurious things

he has, not to those which contribute to his ad-
vantage if he knows the right use of them.
C. We must reject what is hurtful; but outward things
are not injurious.
D. The things which we use badly, and which the Lord
commands us to put away, are the infirmities and
passions of the soul.

XVI. Of this wealth the (infirmities and passions)
A. A man must render his soul pure, that is, pure and
bare, and then only must he listen to the Saviour
when He says, "Come, "follow me."
1. An impure soul is that which is rich in lusts and
in travail with worldly affections.
2. For he who holds possessions as gifts of God
held in trust for his brothers is the man who is
blessed by the Lord and called poor in spirit.

XVII. But he who carries his wealth in his soul—how can
he desire and meditate on the kingdom of heaven?
There are:
A. two kinds of treasure: good and bad.
1. "The good treasure of the heart brings forth that
which is good."
2. "The evil creature brings forth that which is evil."
(Mt.6:45)
B. Also, there is one wealth of good things, another of
evil: the one desirable, the other undesirable.
1. In the same manner also spiritual poverty is
blessed. (Mt. 5:3)

XVIII. We must understand how the disciples used the
word "rich."
A. Salvation does not depend upon the paucity or abun-
dance of outward things, but upon the soul's virtue,
upon faith, etc.
B. Strength and greatness of body do not give life, nor
does insignificance of the limbs destroy, but the
soul provides the cause that leads to richer result.

C. Let us no longer seek for the cause of our end anywhere else except in the character and disposition of the soul with regard to its obedience to God.

XIX. There are two kinds of richness and two kinds of poorness.
A. The truly rich man is rich in virtues; the spurious rich man is rich in the flesh.
1. The former leads to eternal life; the latter to eternal death.
B. The truly poor man is poor in spirit; the spurious poor man is bereft in a worldly sense.
1. The former is blessed; the latter, if rich in lusts and vices, and not poor in spirit, must sell his alien possessions.
C. They may be sold by introducing other riches which deify and give treasure in the heavens.

XX. The rich man, not understanding these things figuratively, went away gloomy and downcast, abandoning the life which he desired, because he made the difficult impossible.
A. Even the disciples are at first filled with fear.
1. They understood and perceived the depth of His words.
2. They also had not completely put away their passions.
B. For salvation belongs to the pure and passionless.

XXI. A man achieves nothing by his own exertions to be freed from his passions, but he attains it by the addition of the power of God
A. To save men against their will is an act of force, but to save them when they choose is an act of grace.
B. Because the kingdom of heaven belongs to those who take it by violence (Mt.11:12)
1. God delights in being vanquished by such things.
C. This is the true following of the Saviour, by aiming at sinlessness and at His perfections, adorning and

regulating the soul before Him after His likeness.

XXII. The God of peace, who exhorts us to love our enemies, does not propose that we should hate and part
from our dearest ones. (Mk 10:29 and Lk 14:26)
   A. The absurdity of a literal understanding of Scripture.
      1. If we love our enemies, how much more are we
         to love our kindred.
      2. Or, if we hate our kindred, how much more ought
         we hate our enemies.
      3. Such statements cancel each other, but such is not
         the case.
   B. In the one saying Christ cuts at the root of hatred, in
      the other of false respect for our kindred, if it is det-
      rimental to salvation.

XXIII. Two appeals presented to you which you must judge
and decide on.
   A. The first is from your earthly father who beckons
      you to follow in his sin, for he begat you for this.
   B. The second is from Christ who gave you new birth
      into a new life and gave His life.
   C. When you have heard these appeals pass judgment
      and vote for your own salvation.

XXIV. If you can cope with your riches then Christ will not
draw you away from them.
   A. But if you know they will beat you, flee from them.

XXV. The meaning of the passage on persecution. (Mk.
10:30)
   A. How one kind of persecution comes from without,
      when men harry the faithful.
   B. But the hardest persecution proceeds from each
      man's soul.
      1. This persecution is harder because it arises from
         within us; we can never escape it.
      2. The same holds true for burning and war. (Rom.
         5:4 and 1 Cor. 6:9)

   C. Choose, before all temporal and separable entities, the Saviour, the advocate and counsel for your soul.

XXVI. Concerning the question before us it must be stated that the promise does not fall short in any respect, because the Saviour has by no means shut out the rich.
   A. That is, provided they are able and willing to stoop beneath God's commandments.
   B. If a man has been banished from life for being born in wealth it is rather he who has been wronged by God who brought him into existence
   C. But if a man can keep his wealth within bounds, here is one who approaches the commandments as a poor man.
     1. If he is unable or unwilling to do so, then it were easier for a camel to enter through the eye of a needle.

XXVII. Let this illustration show (the camel) that the rich (well-to-do) must not neglect their salvation because they feel they are condemned beforehand.
   A. Nor are they to throw their wealth overboard, but must learn how to use it and acquire life.
   B. What hope does the Saviour outline for the rich?
     1. We must love God with our whole being, because it is not reverent to consider any other thing as more venerable: this is the first commandment in the outline.
     2. For in proportion as a man loves God, he enters more closely into God.

XXVIII. A second part of the outline.
   A. "Thou shalt love thy neighbor as thyself" (Mt. 22:39) consequently God above thyself.
   B. "Who is the neighbor?" Explained by the parable of the Good Samaritan. (Lk. 10:9)
   C. We are to do likewise, because love (of God) buds into well-doing.

XXIX. The outline is explained and its meaning broadened.
  A. In both commandments Jesus introduces love, but
      with a distinction in order.
    1. First, the highest form of love is love of God.
    2. Second, the lower form of love is love of our
        neighbor.
  B. Christ is our Samaritan, who heals us of our wounds.
    1. Jesus is the only healer of these wounds because
        he cuts out our passions by the roots.
  C. We are therefore to love him equally with God.
    1. He loves Christ who does His will and keeps His
        commandments.

XXX. Whatever service a man does for a disciple the Lord
      accepts for Himself and reckons it all his own. (Mt.
      25:34-40)
  A. On the other hand, those who do not provide these
      things for them He casts into the eternal fire, on the
      grounds that they have not provided for Him.

XXXI. Those who believe on Him He calls children, in
      comparison with their future greatness above.
  A. The only reward we cannot lose is that which comes
      from receiving others in His name.
  B. The order of this doing: We should not wait to be
      asked, but seek personally after whoever is worthy
      of help, thereby fixing our reward in heaven.

XXXII. What splendid trading! You buy immortality with
      money.
  A. Spare not dangers or toils, that here you may buy a
      heavenly kingdom.
  B. Do not delight in material things, desire to live and
      reign in heaven with God.
  C. The Lord said "make a frIend (of unrighteous mam-
      mon);" and a friend is not made from one gift.
  D. "He that endureth to the end, the same shall be
      saved." (Mt. 10:22)

XXXIII. How is one to give these things?
    A. Do not yourself decide who is worthy and who un-
        worthy, for you may be mistaken.
        1. By being niggardly you may neglect some who
            are beloved of God the penalty for which is eter-
            nal punishment by fire.
    B. Hidden within the material form dwells the Father,
        and His Son. (Jn.14:23)

XXXIV. This form (*schēma*) that is seen deceives death
        and the devil; for the inward wealth and beauty
        are invisible to them.
    A. They do not know the treasure within, which is forti-
        fied by the power of God the Father and the blood
        of God the Son and the dew (*drosō*) of the Holy
        Spirit
    B. Enlist to yourself an army dear God, armed with
        gentleness and love.
        1. Through such an army the attacks of the foe are
            reduced to impotence.

XXXV. Effective soldiers are these, and steadfast guardi-
        ans, not one idle or useless.
    A. They seem not to touch your flesh but each his own
        soul, not to be talking with a brother but with the
        King of the ages who dwells in you.

XXXVI. All the faithful are noble and godlike, but there
        are some who are even more elect than the elect.
    A. These are they who hide in the depth of their mind
        the unutterable mysteries and scorn to let their no-
        bility of nature be seen in the world.
    B. This is the seed, God's image and likeness, sent here
        on a foreign service.
    C. Hierarchy of the visible and invisible created order.
        1. Some created for His service.
        2. Some for training.
        3. Some for instruction.

4. All held together by the seed which remains until
it is gathered in. (cf. *Extracts from Theodotos*
26.3)

XXXVII. What else is necessary? Behold the mysteries of
love, for God in His very self is love and for
love's sake becomes visible to us.
  A. While the unspeakable part of Him is Father, the part
  that has sympathy with us is Mother.
  B. This is why the Son Himself came to earth, that He
  might measure us to His own power.
    1. He leaves us a New Testament, "I give you my
    love." (Jn. 13:34; 14:27)
  C. He laid down His life for us and in return demands
  this sacrifice from us on behalf of one another.
    1. Shall we then still husband and hoard up the
    things of this world?
  D. Divine indeed is the saying of John: "He that loveth
  not his brother is a murderer." (1 Jn. 3:15)

XXXVIII. Learn the more excellent way to salvation
which Paul shows. (1 Cor. 12:31)
  A. "Love does not seek its own" (1 Cor. 13:5), but is
  lavished upon the brother.
  B. Faith goes away, when we persuade ourselves by a
  vision to see God.
    1. Hope vanishes when we are granted what we
    have hoped for.
    2. Love goes with us into God's presence and in-
    creases when the perfect is bestowed.
  C. Even though a man be born in sins, if he but implant
  love in his soul he is is able to retrieve his failures.

XXXIX. (Taken from Butterworth) If you understand how
a man may use his substance to win life—even
though he happened to fall after his redemption
—let not this thought remain with you, that such

a one has been condemned outright by God.
  A. Genuine repentance is to utterly root out the sins
     which for which a man has condemned himself to
     death.
     1. When these (sins) are destroyed God will enter
        and dwell in you.
  B. God waits for those who turn to Him and to turn to
     Him is to cease from our sins and look back no
     more.

     (Coxe has a strikingly different translation
     of the first line, which reads . . . "If one
     should escape the superfluity of riches . . .
     but should happen, either from ignorance or
     involuntary circumstances, after . . . redemp-
     tion, to fall into sins . . . such a man is reject-
     ed by God." The reader may wish to consult
     the Greek text in either the Loeb Classical
     Library or Texts and Studies, vol. 5, n. 2., in
     order to resolve the difference for himself.)

XL. God gives forgiveness of past sins, but of future
    sins each man procures his own remission.
  A. This is repentance, to condemn the deeds that are
     past and to ask forgetfulness of them from the Fa-
     ther.
  B. Even when a man lives faithfully all his life, but falls
     at the end, all his former labors bring him no profit.
     1. Whereas he who has led an indifferent life, may,
        if he repents, utterly wipe out a wicked course.
  C. Repress the passions in order that at your departure
     you may be found to have already become recon-
     ciled with your adversary. (Mt. 5:25)
  D. With sincere repentance and constant practice suc-
     cess is achieved.

XLI. You who are rich should appoint some man of God as
     your trainer.
  A. You must react to his anger and groaning with fear

and grief.
  1. Let him be your ambassador with God, for God
     listens to his children who beg His mercies.
  B. This man will beg them, if he is sincerely honored
     by you and in nothing grieved by you, but only for
     you.
     1. This is unfeigned repentance.
  C. For God alone discerns the heart's intent; and is near
     to all believers.

XLII. To give you confidence when you have thus truly re-
     pented, hear a true story about St. John and the rob-
     ber.
  A. St John was traveling among the Churches in the en-
     virons of Ephesus.
     1. In a particular town he noticed a certain youth,
        whom he entrusted to the care of the bishop of
        that place.
     2. The presbyter took the youth home, brought him
        up, and enlightened him by baptism.
     3. The youth became an idler and organized a band
        of robbers.
     4. St. John on his return inquired about the youth;
        when told of his fall he pursued him.
     5. His imprecations and pleadings caused the youth
        to repent and, with the intercedings of St. John,
        on his behalf, to return to the church.
  B. A lacuna appears at this point.
  C. And before them all the Saviour comes to meet him,
     leading him to the Father's bosom, to eternal life.
  D. In this let a man trust to the authority of the gospels
     and the words of the apostles.
     1. Then He will see at the moment of death the
        proof of the doctrines.
  E. But if a man chooses to remain in pleasures, sinning
     time after time, let him blame his own soul for his
     damnation.
  F. He who looks for salvation with importunity and vio-
     lence shall receive the true purification.